THE COLORS

FIELD OF JOY

-STEVEN STENZLER-

First Edition: September 2024

ISBN: 979-8-89397-252-8

Published by AMZ Kindle Direct Publications

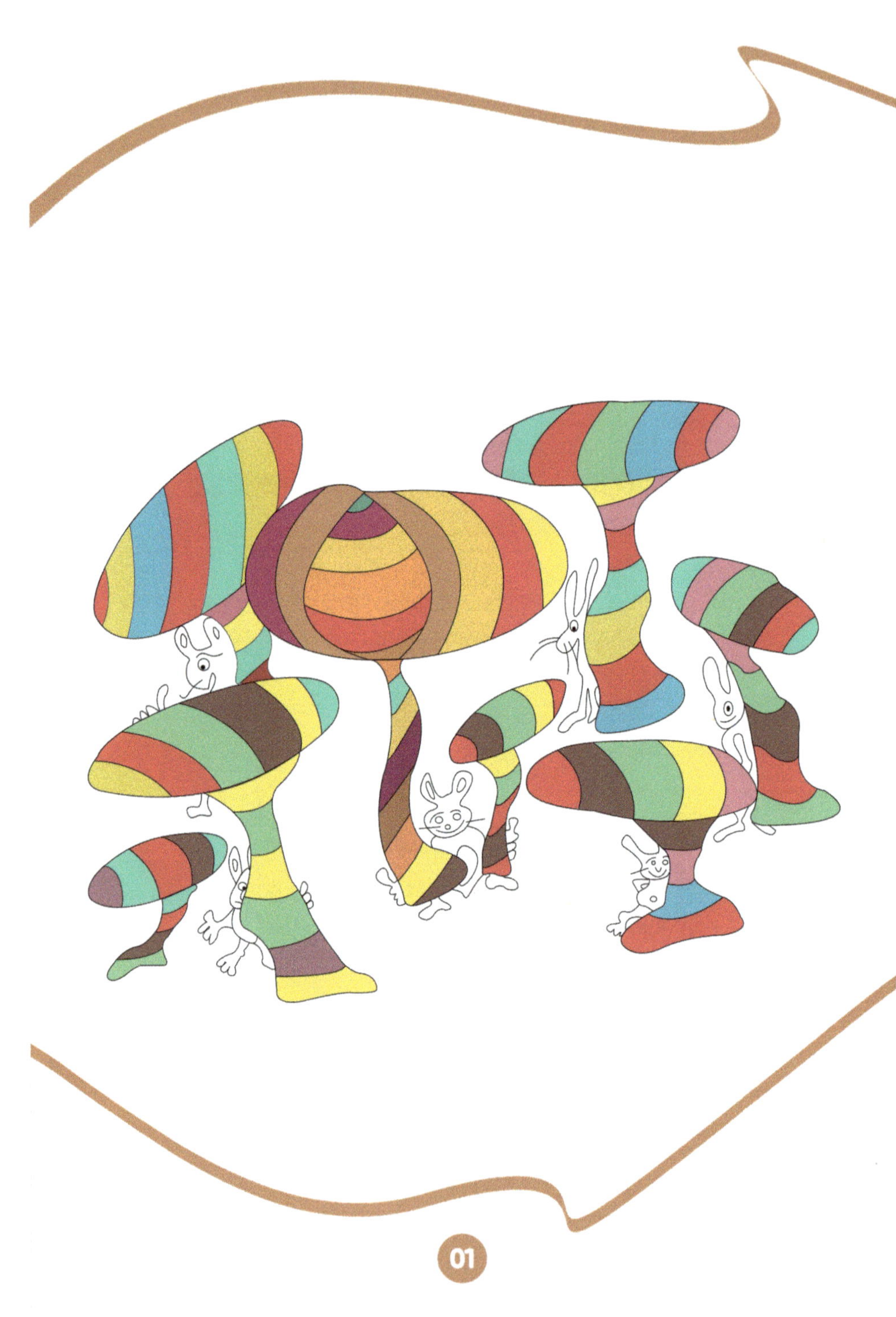

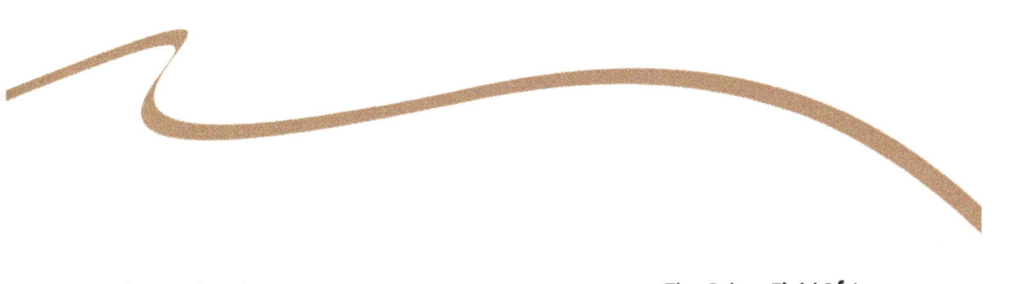

WHERE HAVE ALL THE RABBITS GONE? LOOK CLOSELY—THEY'RE HIDING PLAYFULLY AMONG THE COLORFUL, STRIPED MUSHROOMS, BLENDING IN WITH THEIR VIBRANT SURROUNDINGS!

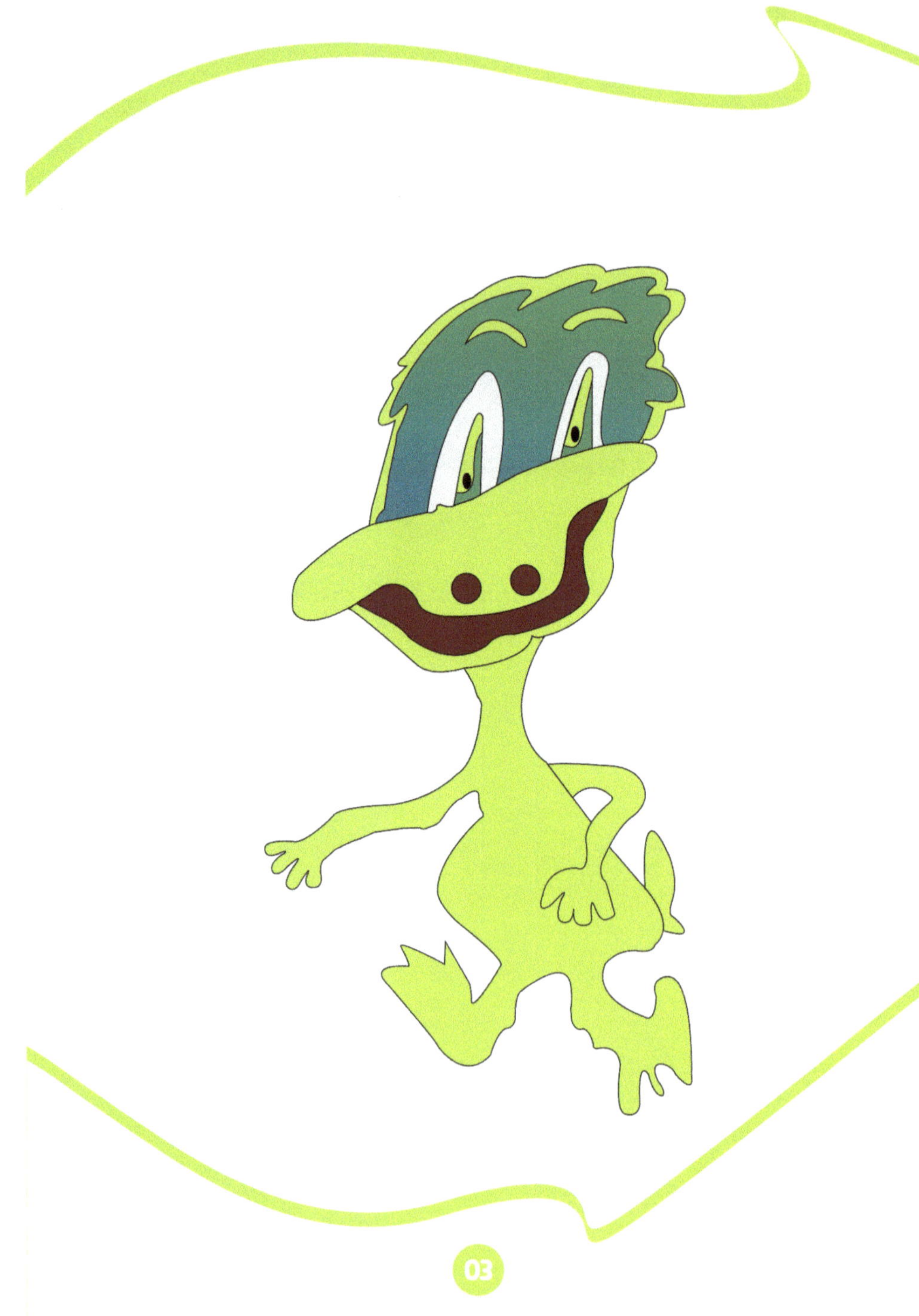

GREENISH DUCKY, IT'S PERFECTLY OKAY TO BE CHARTREUSE! EMBRACE YOUR UNIQUE, BRIGHT COLOR–AFTER ALL, IT'S WHAT MAKES YOU STAND OUT AND SHINE IN YOUR OWN SPECIAL WAY!

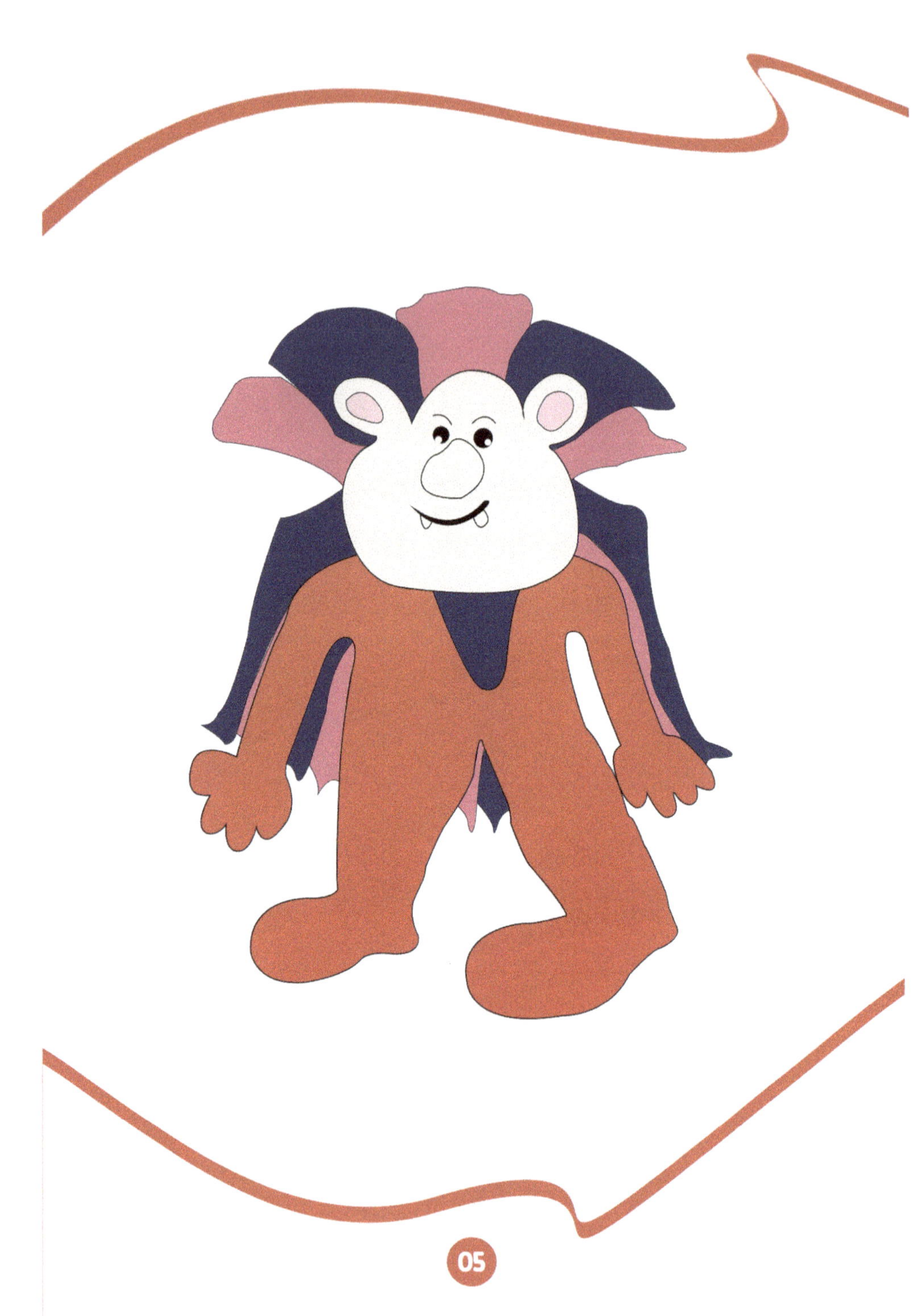

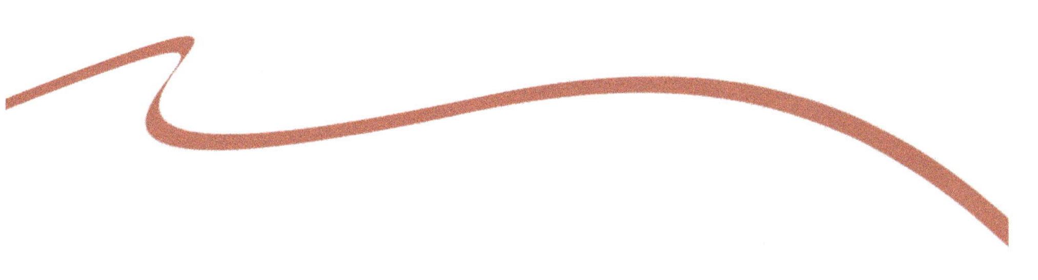

YES, YOU GUESSED IT—I AM INDEED A COUNT! WITH MY FANGS AND CAPE,

I'M READY TO BRING SOME SPOOKY FUN, BUT DON'T WORRY,

I'M MORE FRIENDLY THAN FRIGHTENING!

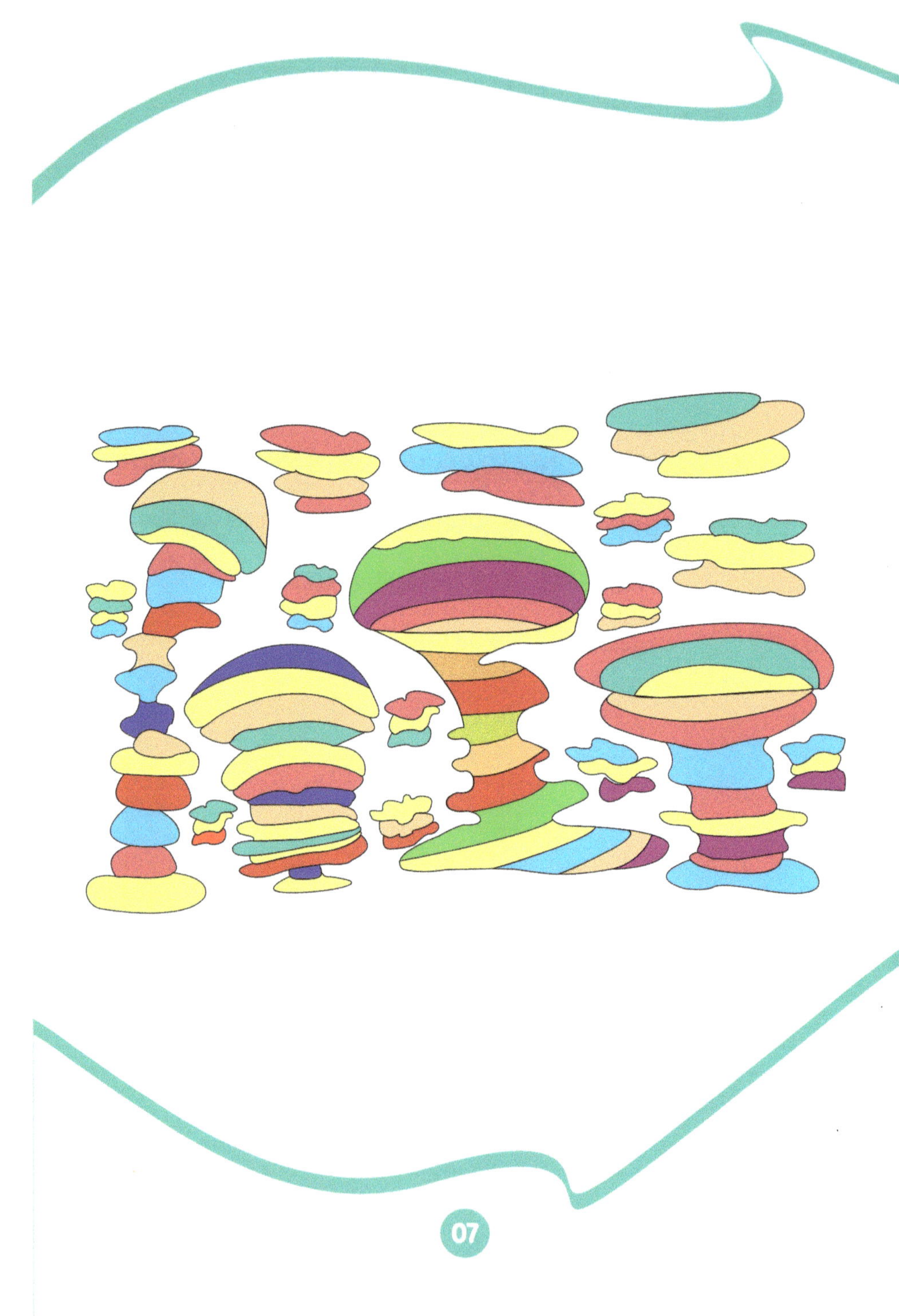

"LOOK UP IN THE SKY AND LET YOUR HEART DELIGHT IN THE VIBRANT COLORS OF JOY! EACH HUE DANCES PLAYFULLY IN THE CLOUDS, PAINTING THE WORLD WITH A RAINBOW OF HAPPINESS AND WONDER."

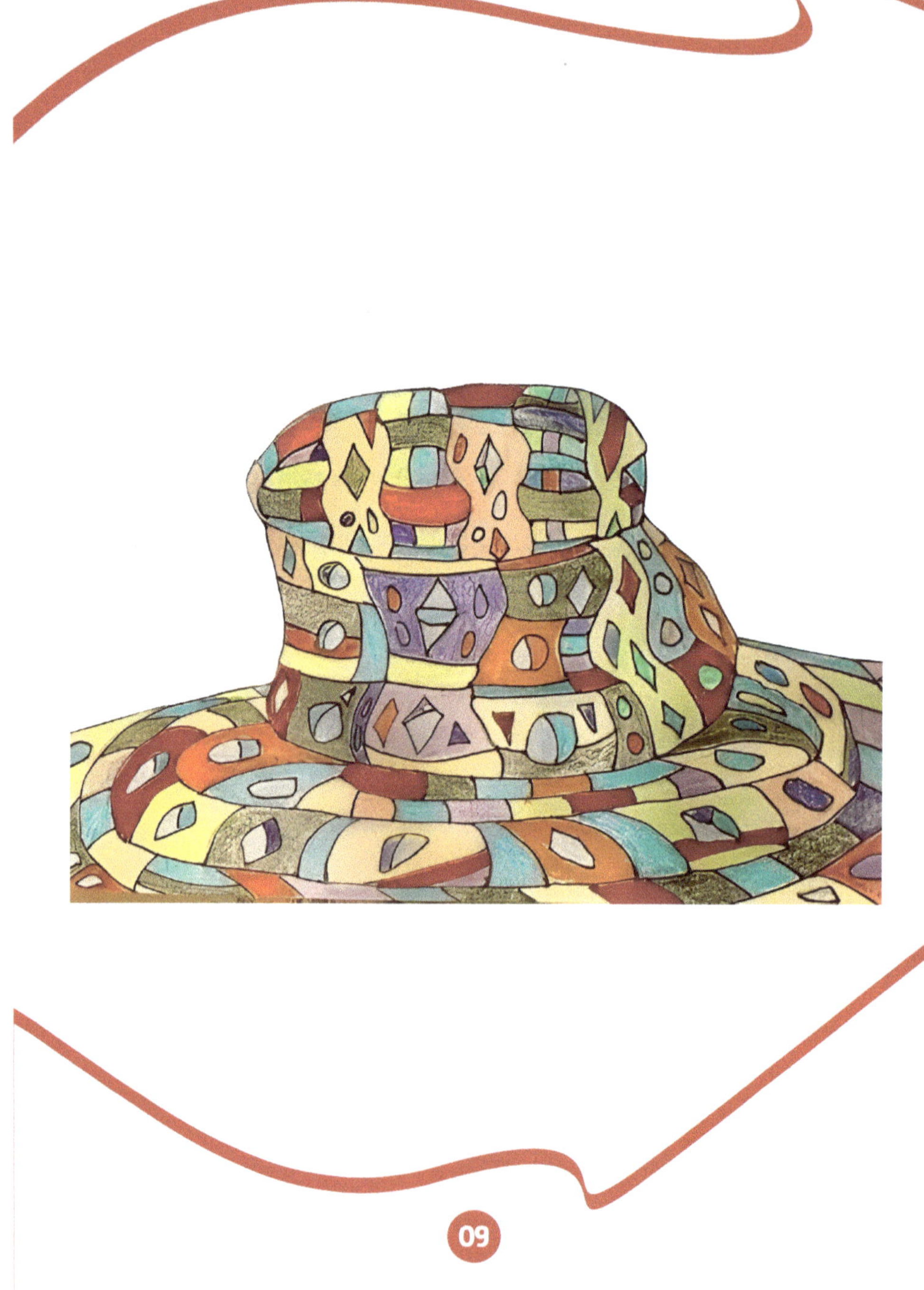

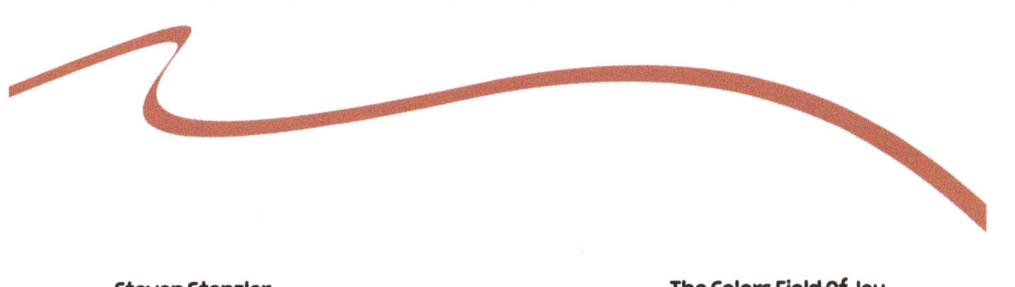

"THE MOTHERSHIP BECKONS YOU ABOARD, WHERE ENDLESS WONDERS AWAIT YOUR CURIOUS MIND. PREPARE FOR A JOURNEY WHERE GRAVITY ITSELF MIGHT KEEP YOU FLOATING, EXPLORING THE COLORFUL MYSTERIES THAT LIE BEYOND!"

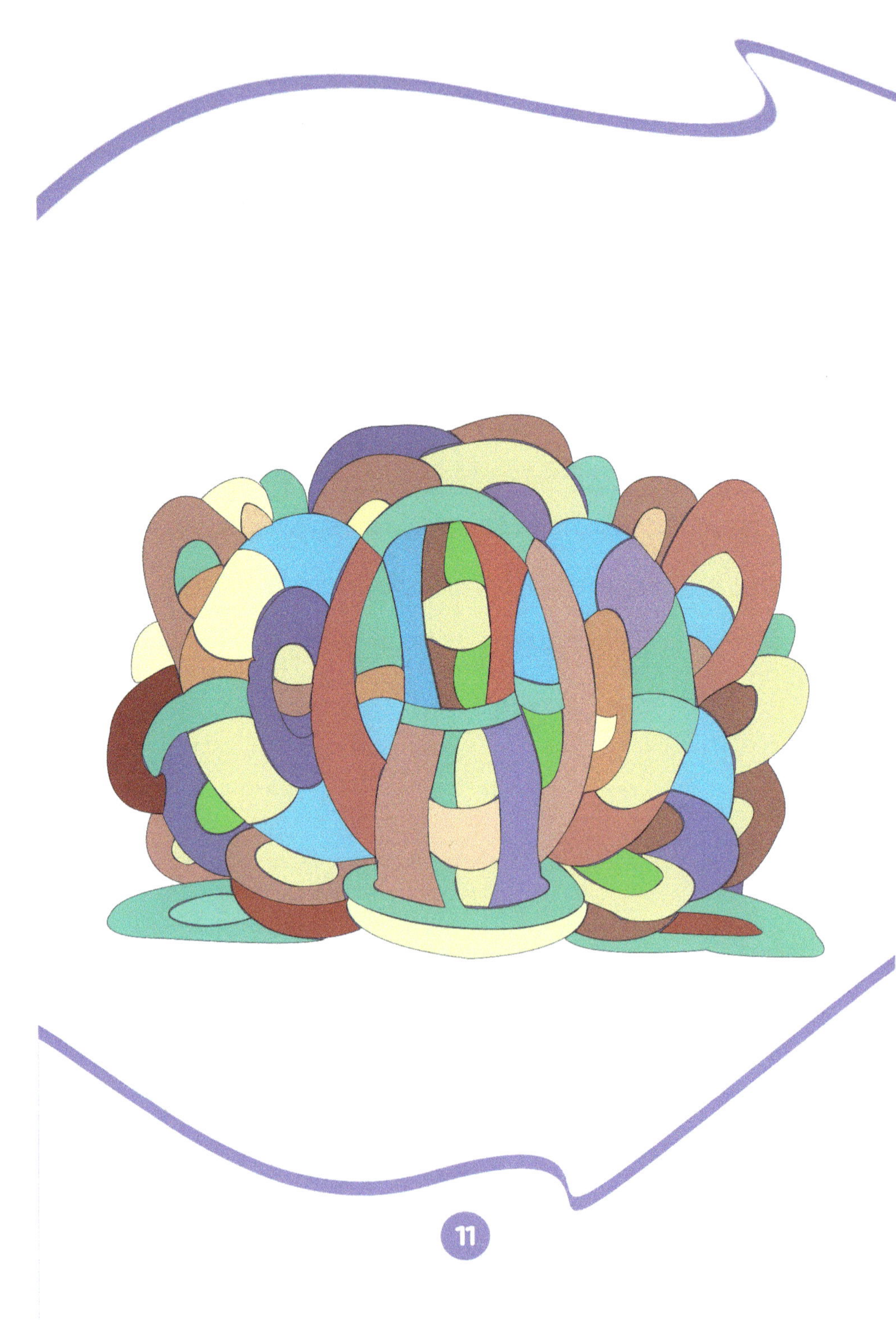

"DEEP WITHIN THIS VIBRANT MAZE, THE COLOR KEEPER WAITS FOR YOU TO EXPLORE. DIVE INTO THE TANGLE OF HUES AND SHAPES, & UNCOVER THE SECRETS HIDDEN IN ITS COLORFUL CORE!"

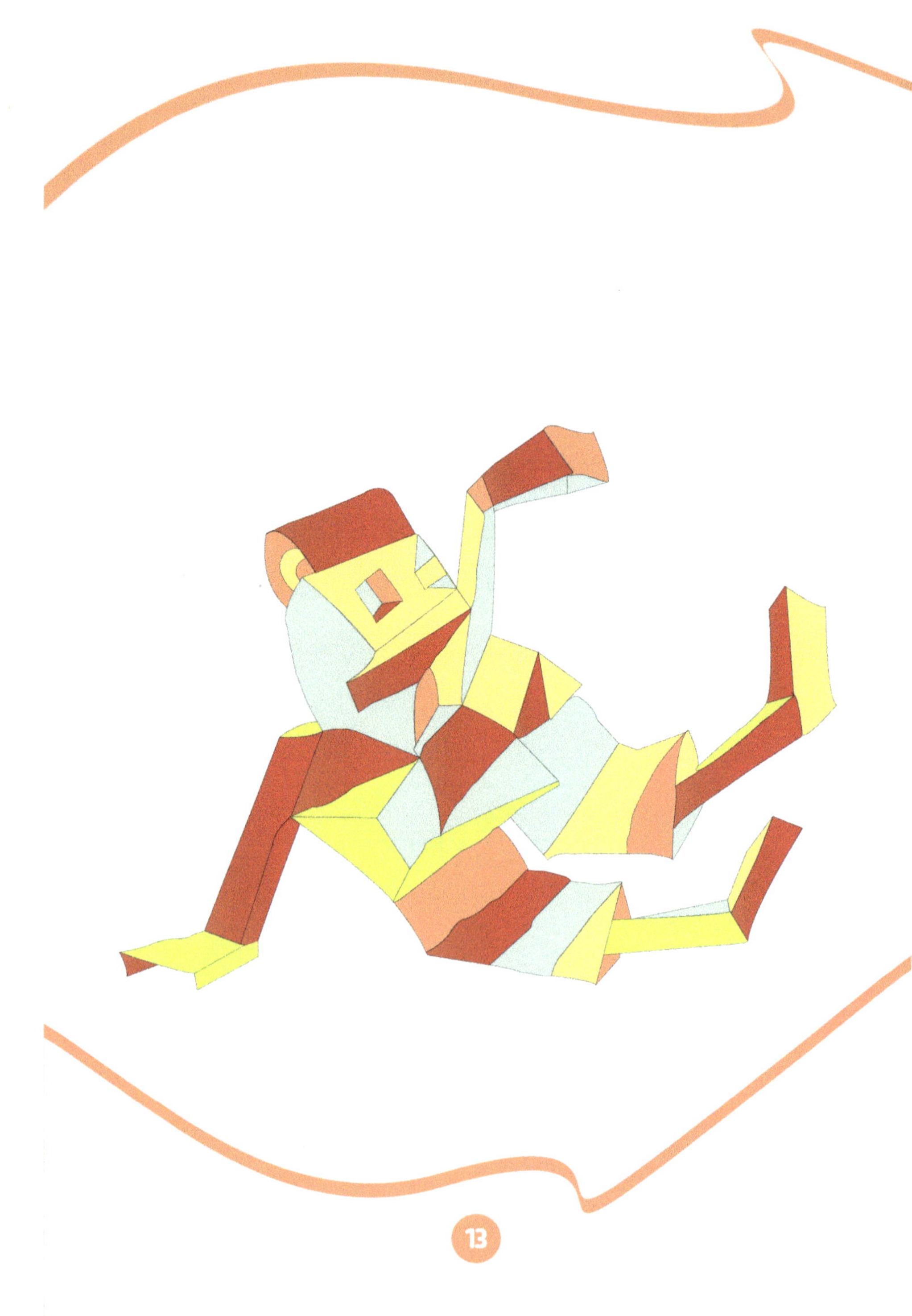

OOPS! THE ROBOT TAKES A TUMBLE BUT STILL SHINES BRIGHTLY WITH ITS BEAUTIFUL, COLORFUL PATTERNS. EVEN IN ITS FALL, THE ROBOT'S VIBRANT COLORS REMAIN AS LIVELY AS EVER!

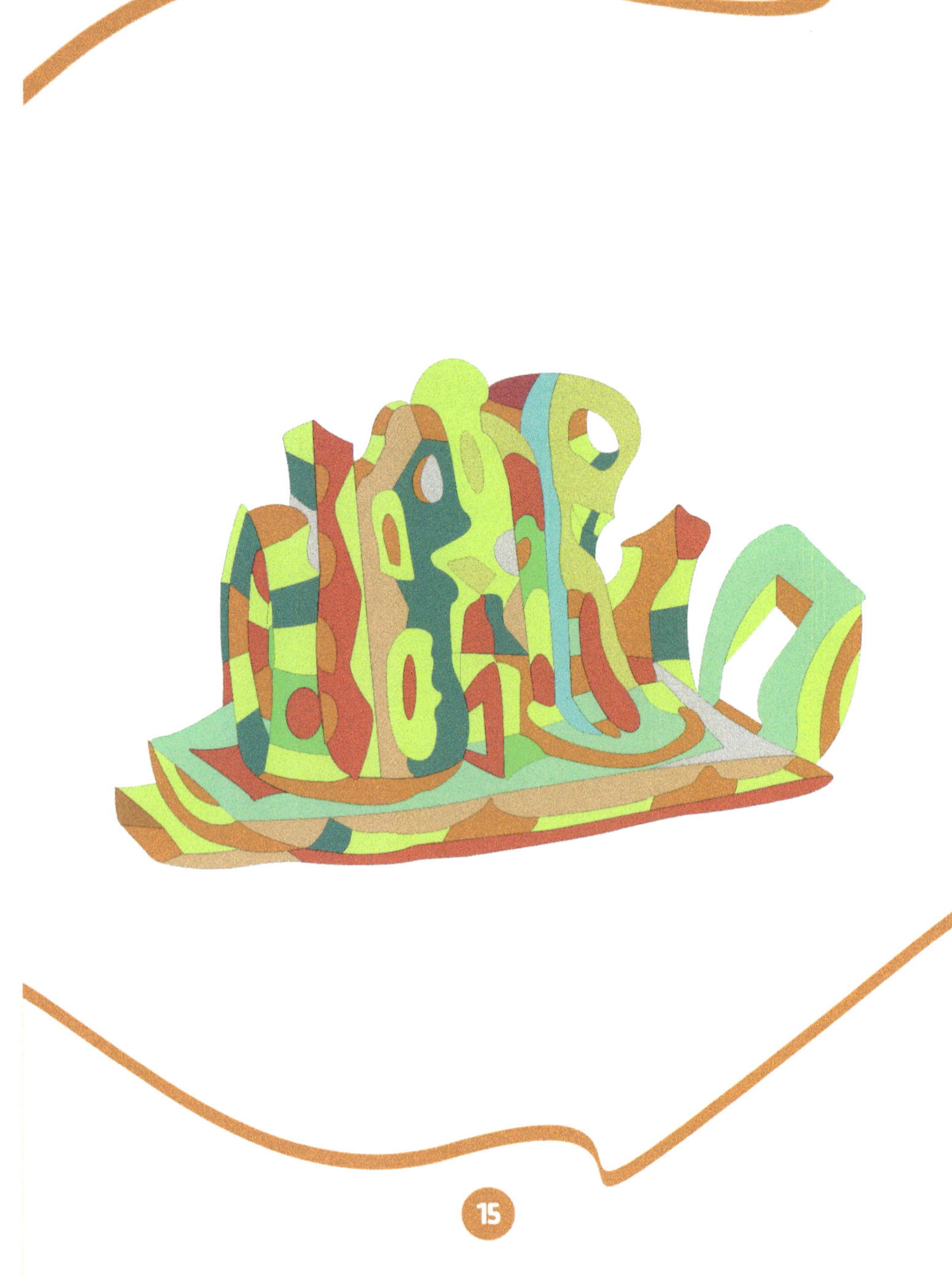

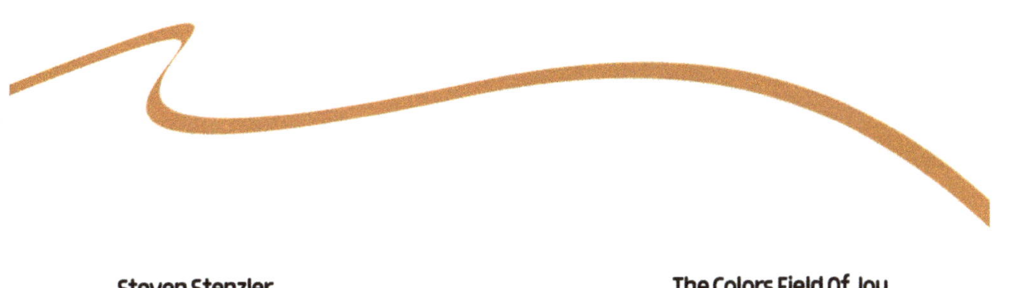

JOIN THE CROWD ON THE WAVES OF MYSTICAL ADVENTURES ACROSS THE SEVEN SEAS.

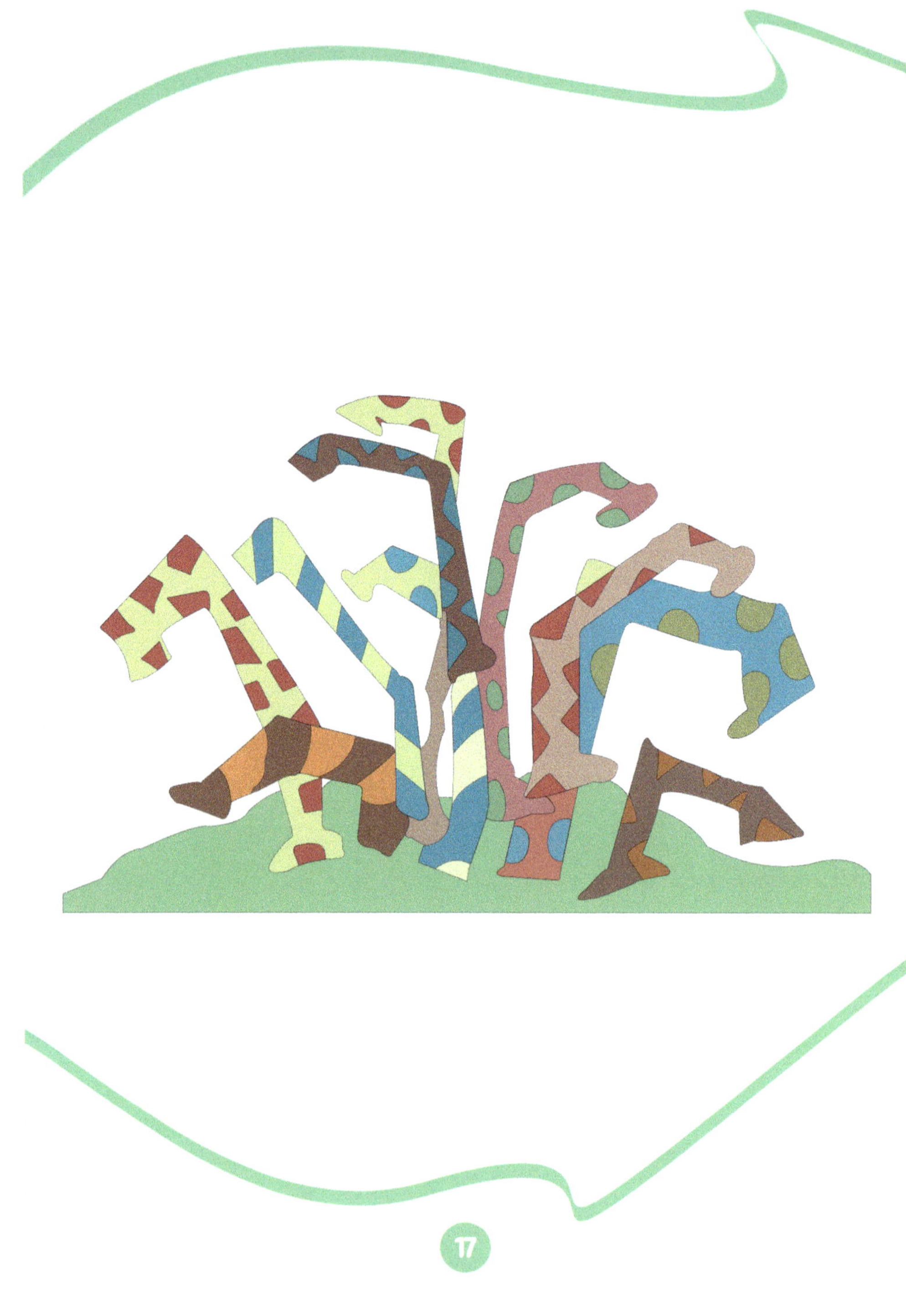

"WOW, THE VIBRANT COLORS CALL OUT TO YOU FROM THE KNOLL OF PARADISE AND SPLENDOR. EACH HUE INVITES YOU TO STEP INTO A WORLD OF WONDER, WHERE BEAUTY AND JOY ABOUND IN EVERY CORNER!"

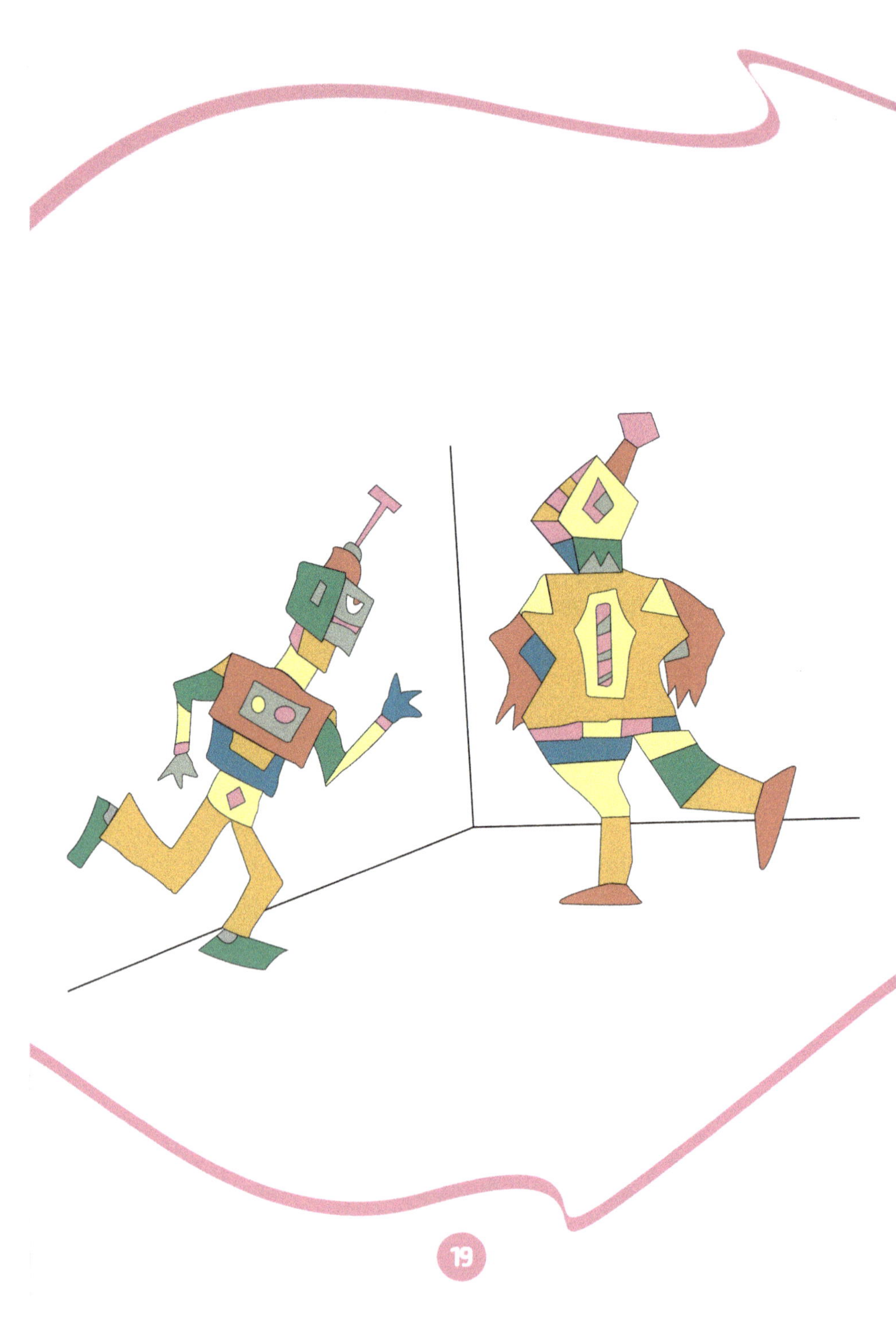

"THE STYLISH DANCE OF THE ROBOTS KEEPS YOU MESMERIZED WITH EVERY MOVE. THEIR VIBRANT COLORS AND RHYTHMIC STEPS ENSURE YOU STAY ENTRANCED, CAPTIVATED BY THEIR PLAYFUL ENERGY & CHARM!"

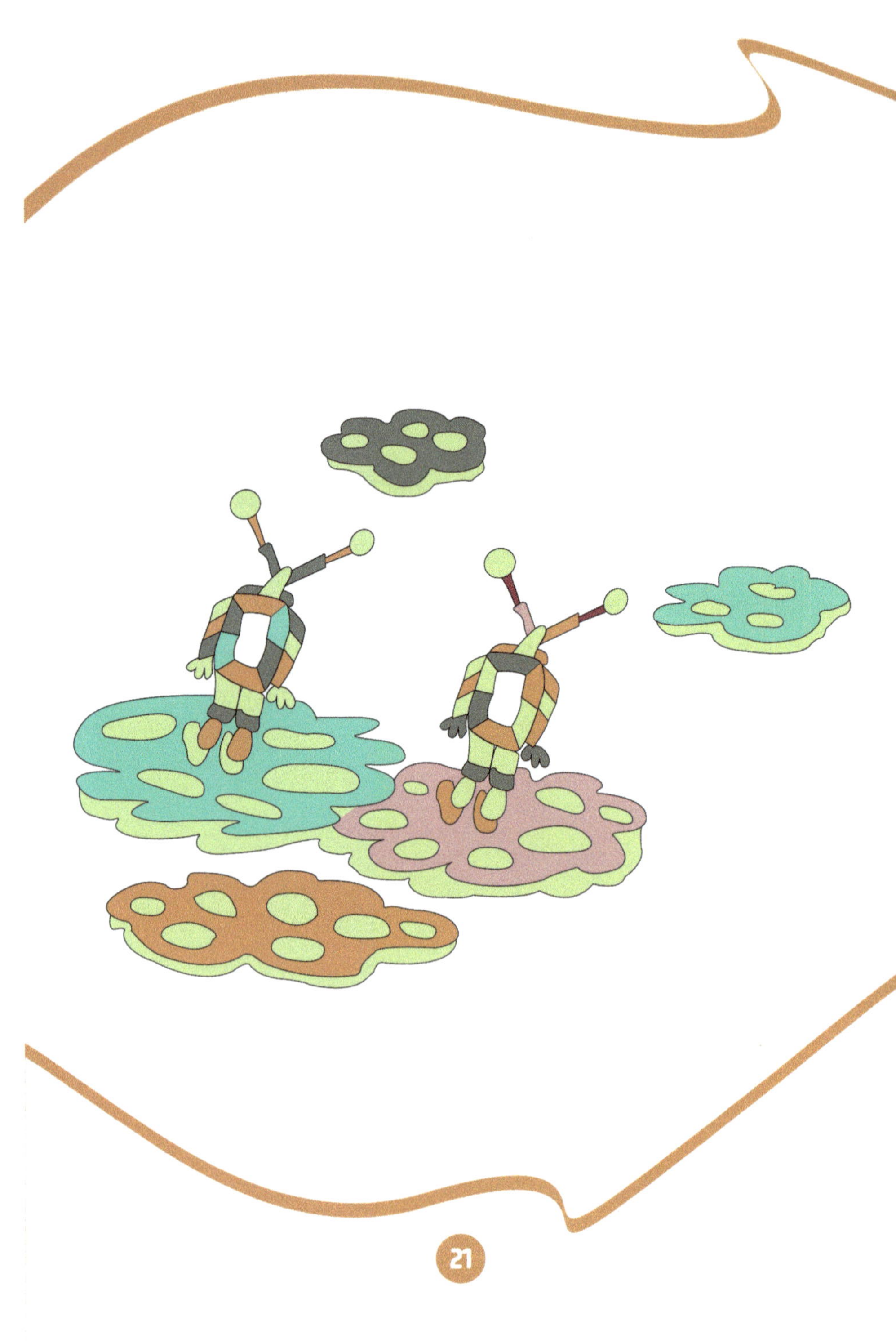

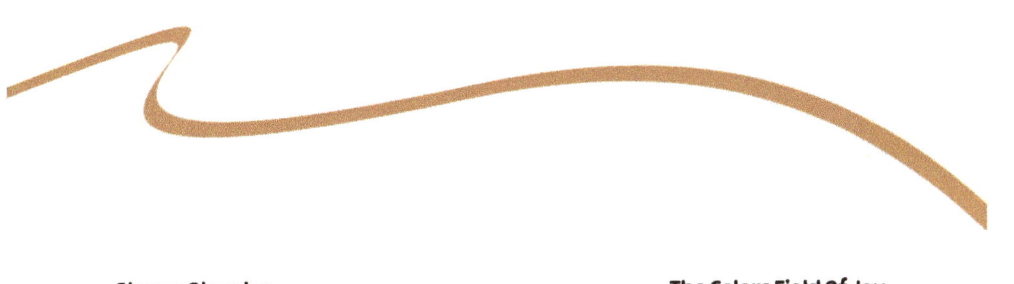

"MYSTERIES AWAIT ALL THE CURIOUS SOULS WHO DARE TO EXPLORE. STEP INTO THE UNKNOWN, WHERE EACH DISCOVERY UNRAVELS NEW WONDERS AND SPARKS THE IMAGINATION!"

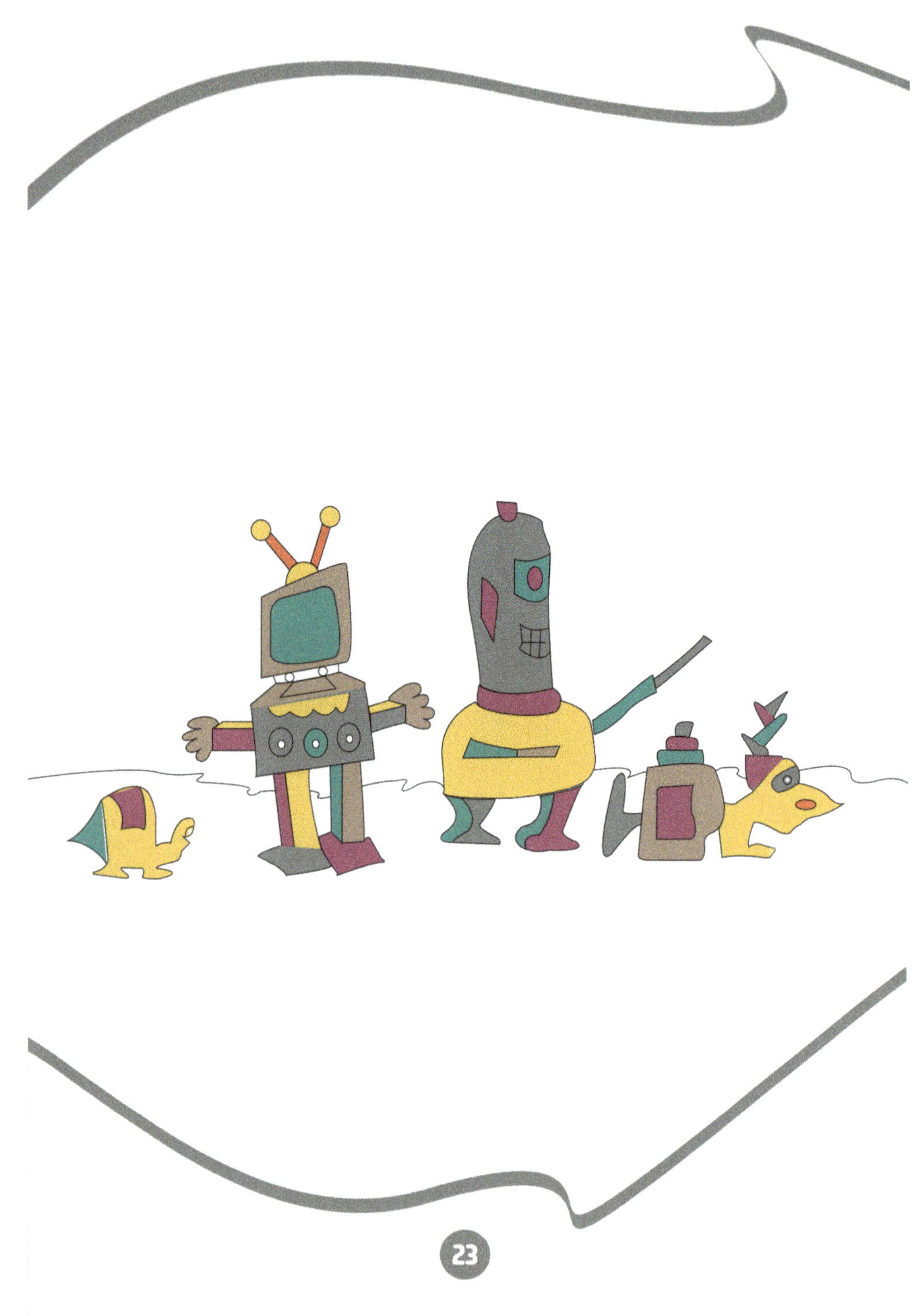

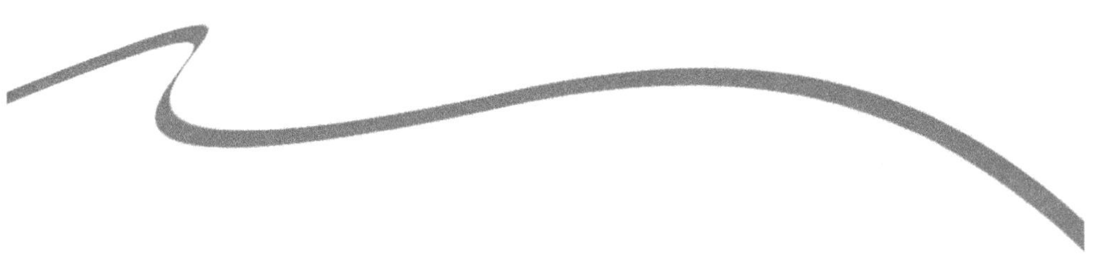

"COME ON, FOLKS! JOIN IN THE FUN—I KNOW YOU'LL ENJOY OUR COLORFUL PARADE. WITH EVERY STEP & SMILE, WE BRING JOY & EXCITEMENT TO EVERYONE WE MEET!"

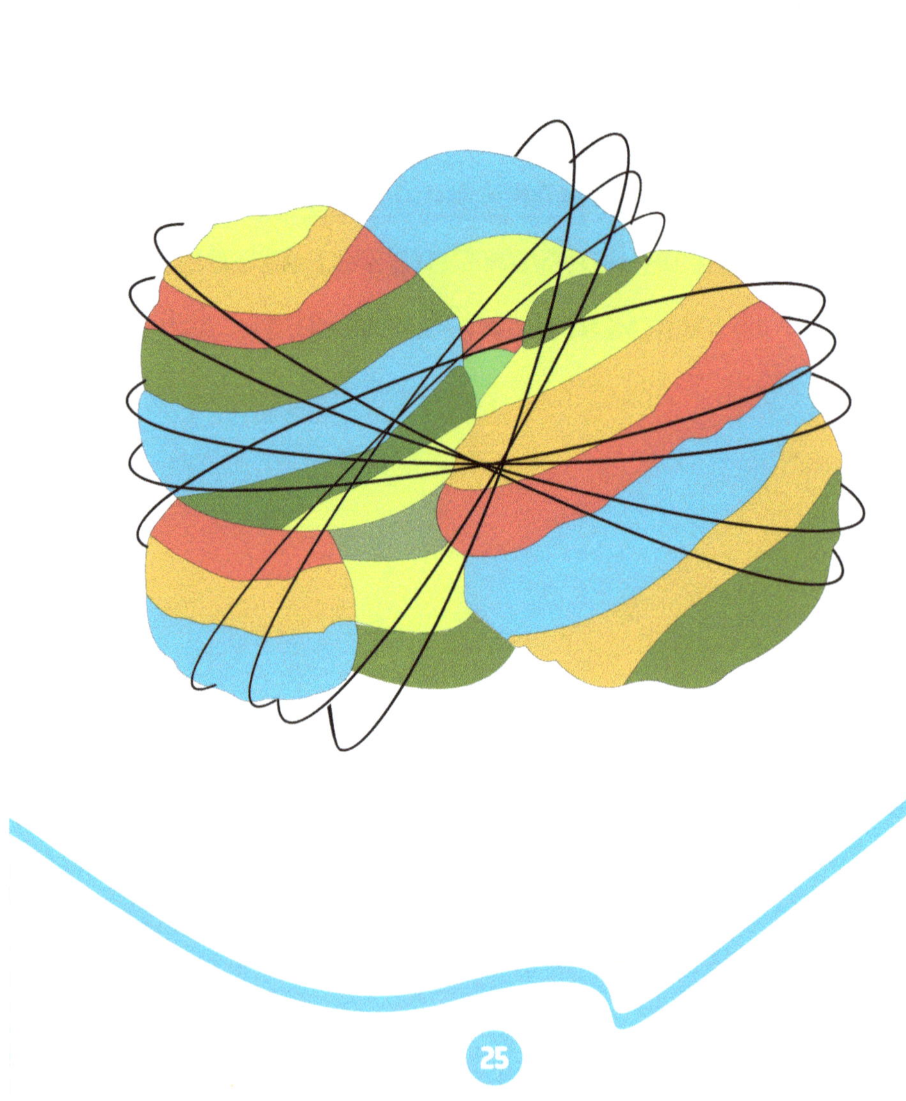

"TEMPORARILY CAUGHT IN THE CELESTIAL REALM OF COLORFUL GASES, YOU FIND YOURSELF SURROUNDED BY SWIRLING HUES OF VIBRANT ENERGY. IT'S A MOMENT OF PURE WONDER, WHERE THE UNIVERSE WRAPS YOU IN ITS MESMERIZING EMBRACE."

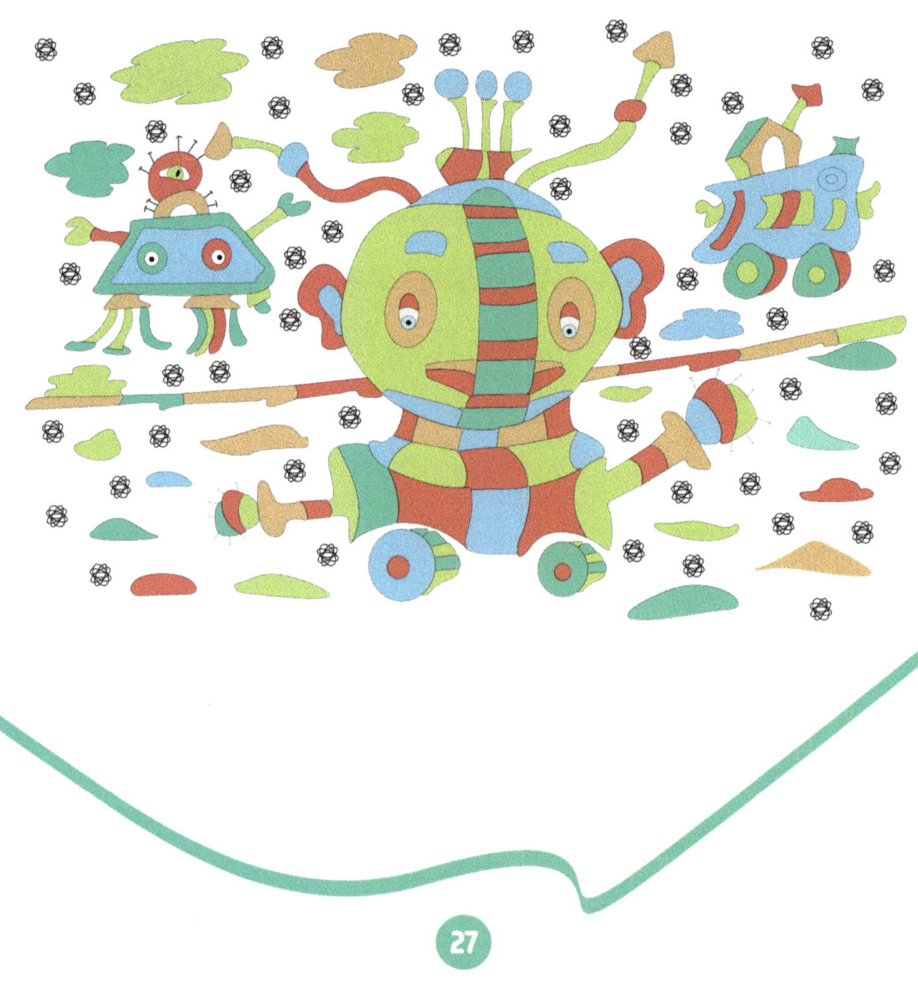

"OH YES, THE HEAVENLY CIRCUS HAS ARRIVED IN YOUR TOWN, BRINGING JOY & WONDER TO ALL! FREE TICKETS ARE ALWAYS AVAILABLE–COME & ENJOY THE WHIMSICAL SHOW OF COLORS, LAUGHTER, & DELIGHT!"

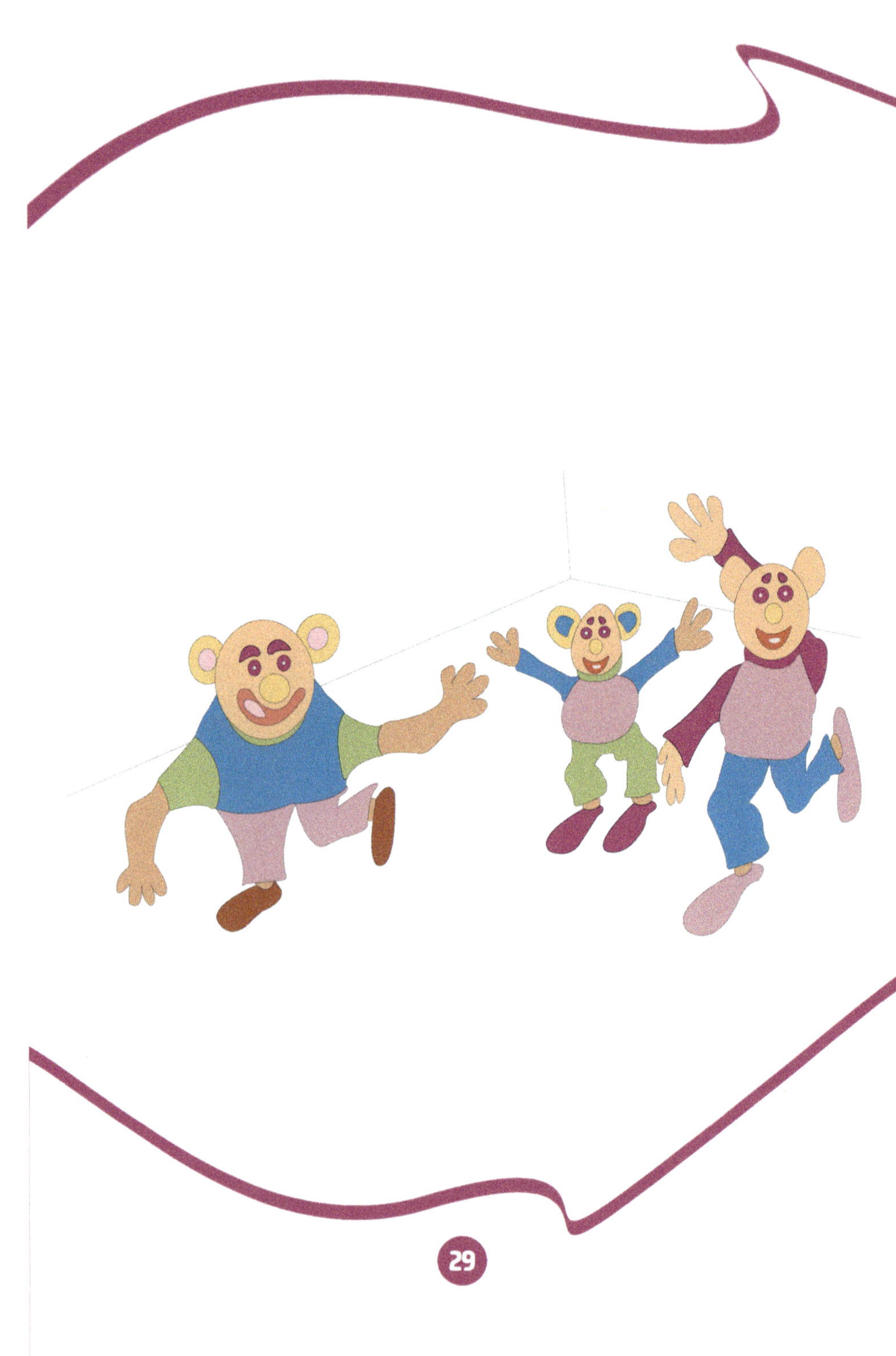

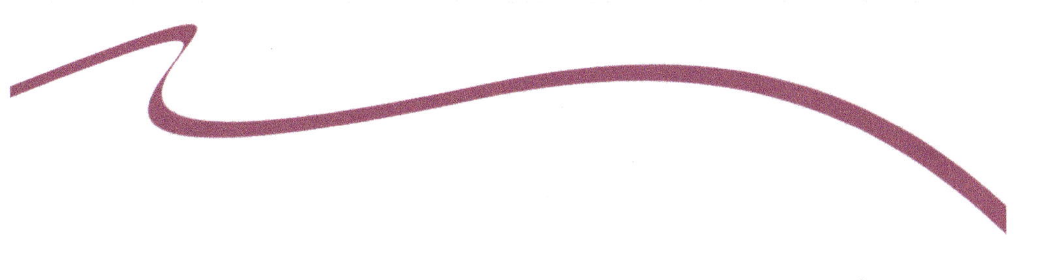

"WE'RE SO EXCITED JUST TO BE—FULL OF JOY & ENERGY, READY TO DANCE & PLAY! EVERY MOMENT IS A CELEBRATION OF THE SIMPLE HAPPINESS THAT FILLS OUR HEARTS."

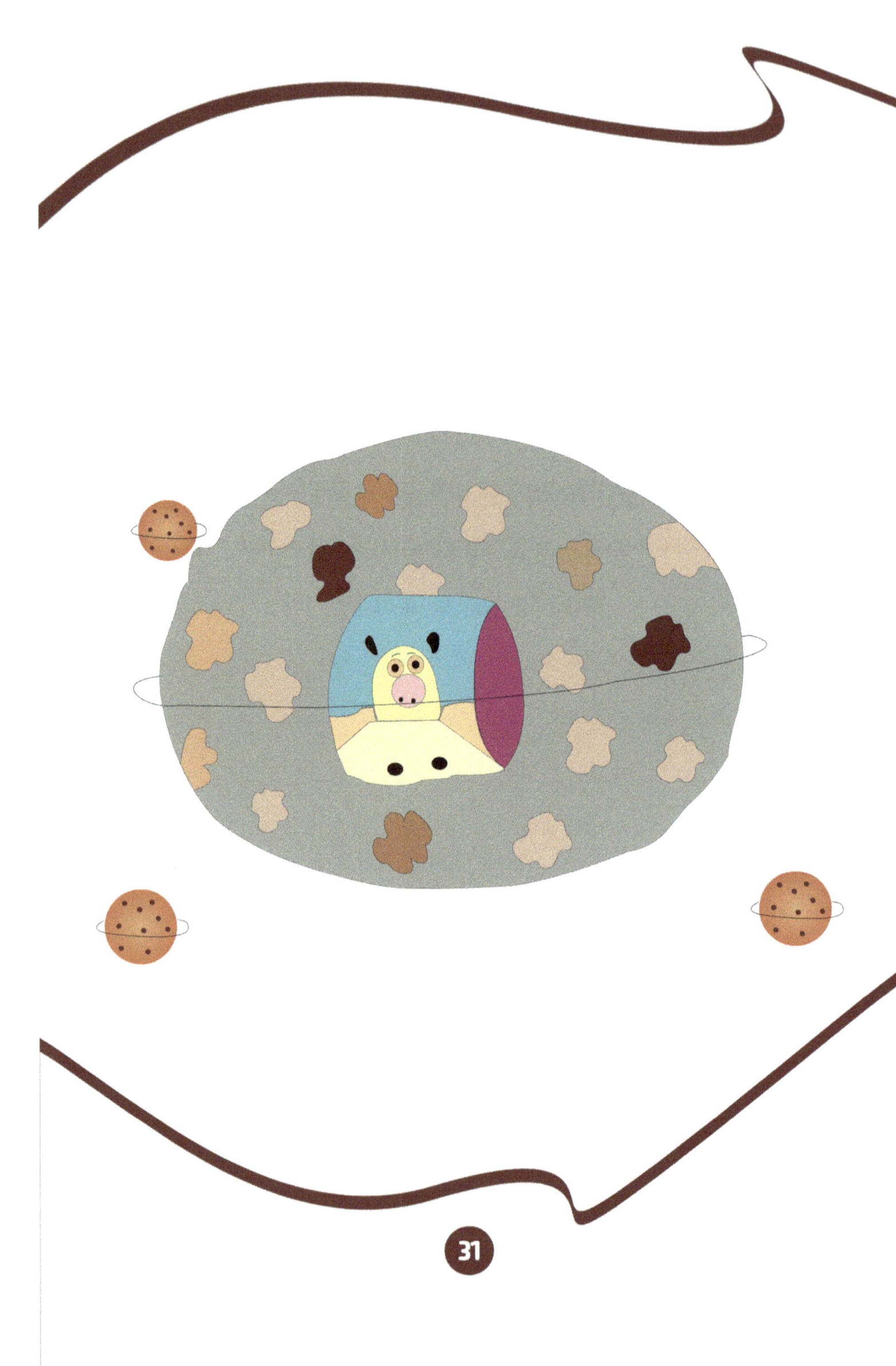

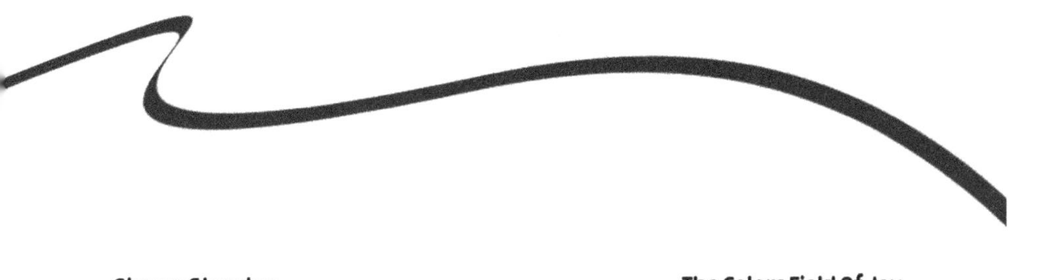

"ONE NEVER KNOWS WHAT MYSTERIES AWAIT IN THE FAR REACHES OF SPACE. OUT THERE IN THE VAST UNKNOWN, ENDLESS POSSIBILITIES & WONDERS ARE JUST WAITING TO BE DISCOVERED."

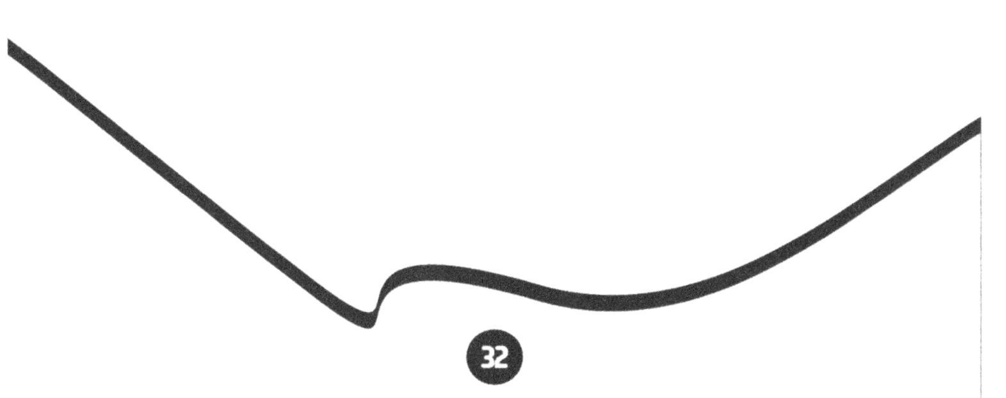

THE END